3rd Grade ELA
Volume 5

© 2013 OnBoard Academics, Inc
Newburyport, MA 01950
800-596-3175
www.onboardacademics.com

ISBN:1494866439

ALL RIGHTS RESERVED. This book contains material protected under International and Federal Copyright Laws and Treaties. Any unauthorized reprint or use of this material is prohibited. No part of this book may be reproduced or transmitted in any form or by any means, electronic or mechanical, including photocopying, recording, or by any information storage and retrieval system without express written permission from the author / publisher. The author grants teacher the right to print copies for their students. This is limited to students that the teacher teachers directly. This permission to print is strictly limited and under no circumstances can copies may be made for use by other teachers, parents or persons who are not students of the book's owner.

Table of Contents

Subject Verb Agreement   4
Subject Verb Agreement Quiz   13
Plural Nouns   14
Plural Nouns Quiz   20
Suffixes and Spelling   21
Suffixes and Spelling Quiz   29
Fluency   30
Fluency Quiz   35

Subject Verb Agreement

Key Vocabulary

subject

verb

helping verb

> **Some verbs do not show action; they show a state of being.**

Underline the verb in each sentence.

The boy scored a goal.

He is excited.

OnBoard Academics Workbook
Grade 3 ELA

Using the verbs on at the bottom of the chart, complete the conjugation chart by filling in all of the boxes.

Pick a verb from each tense and write a sentence using that verb.

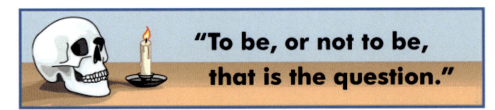
"To be, or not to be, that is the question."

present tense		past tense		future tense	
singular	**plural**	**singular**	**plural**	**singular**	**plural**
I	we are	I was	we were	I will be	we
you are	you	you	you	you	you will be
he/she is	they	he/she was	they	he/she will be	they will be

am   is   are   was   were   will be

_____

Complete the sentences with the present tense of the verb to be.

We [ ] putting on a play.

Jenna [ ] the main character.

I [ ] making the costumes.

We [ ] very excited for the show.

Our families [ ] here to watch.

[am]   [is]   [are]

Fill in the blanks with the past tense of the verb to be.

> **The verbs was and were show the *past tense* of the verb to be and must agree in number with the subject of the sentence.**

I _____ sleepy this morning.

We _____ out late watching a movie.

There _____ green monsters in it.

It _____ very scary.

Find the missing verb and decide if it is singular or plural.
The first one is done for you as an example.

| am | is | are | was | were | S | P |

1. My class **is** studying dinosaurs. **S**
2. I ☐ excited to learn about them. ☐
3. Some species ☐ as small as chickens. ☐
4. The T-Rex ☐ a meat eater. ☐
5. The dinosaurs ☐ extinct. ☐

Helping Verbs

Helping verbs add detail to the way in which time is conveyed in a sentence. They are called helping verbs because they help other verbs show past tense, present tense or future tense.

Read the following sentences.
The sentences are organized by past, present and future. What is the difference between the first group and the second group?

_____

_____

Alison has cleaned her room.

Alison is cleaning her room.

Alison will clean her room.

The boys have helped her.

The boys are helping her.

The boys will help her.

Circle the correct helping verb.

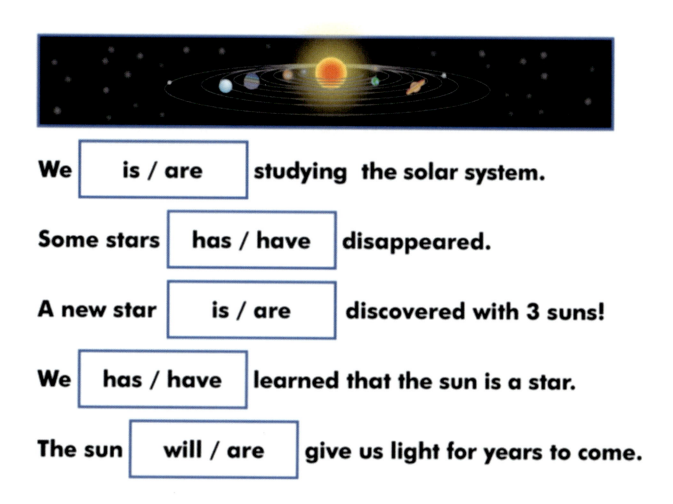

We [is / are] studying the solar system.

Some stars [has / have] disappeared.

A new star [is / are] discovered with 3 suns!

We [has / have] learned that the sun is a star.

The sun [will / are] give us light for years to come.

Subject Verb Agreement

> **Singular** subjects need **singular** verbs and **plural** subjects need **plural** verbs.

Put a check mark in the box next to the sentences that have subject verb agreement.

- ☐ Tory's teacher have finished handing out science reports.

- ☐ Tory was delighted with her science report.

- ☐ David will have a lot of explaining to do when he gets home.

- ☐ Owen's mom and dad is not happy with his report.

- ☐ The principal and vice principal was giving awards for the best reports.

- ☐ Jenna was given one of the awards.

Name_____

Subject Verb Agreement Quiz

1. The helping verb has is used with singular nouns. True or false?
2. Fred _____ washed the car. Circle the answer. was have has is.
3. We _____ going on a picnic. Circle the answer. are have has is
4. We _____ a new baby sister. Circle the answer. was have is were
5. The nurse _____ taking my temperature. Circle the answer. were have is has
6. The bicycle _____ a basket on the front. Circle the answer. has have is was
7. They _____ friendly kittens. Circle the answer. has were is was
8. My friends _____ all there too. Circle the answer. was have is were

Plural Nouns

Key Vocabulary

singular

plural

noun

Plural Nouns

Many plural nouns have an -s at the end.

Add an -es to nouns which end in -ch, -sh, -s, -x or -z to make them plural.

Some special nouns do not follow any rules. They have *irregular* plurals.

Make these nouns plural.

 dog _____

 fox _____

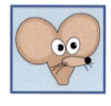 mouse _____

OnBoard Academics Workbook

Grade 3 ELA

How would you change each noun to its plural?
Use the answers s, es, ! as listed below for your answers.

1	book
2	tooth
3	grass
4	cup
5	itch
6	woman

s add -s   **es** add -es   **!** irregular

Nouns that end in 'Y'

Notice how the word changes when you make it plural.

  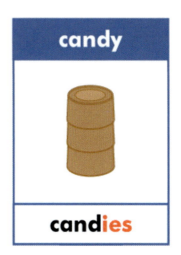

For nouns that end in -y:
"Change the y to i and add es!"

OnBoard Academics Workbook — Grade 3 ELA

Make these nouns plural by adding s, es or ies.
Cross off letters when necessary.

1. cake
2. penny
3. door
4. church
5. city
6. box
7. lady

Underline the incorrect plurals.

My Favorite Thinges
by Tori Kennedy

Sunny skys and sandy beaches

Homemade fries and Georgia peachies.

Friends and familys, cats and dogs

Me and James catching froges.

Bedtime storys then counting sheep,

Goodnight kissies, it's time to sleep.

OnBoard Academics Workbook Grade 3 ELA

Name_____

Plural Nouns Quiz

1. To make a noun plural, you always just add an s. True or false?

2. What is the plural form of party? _____

3. What is the plural form of goose? _____

4. What is the plural form of child? _____

5. What is the plural form of apple? _____

6. What is the plural form of box? _____

7. What is the plural form of candy? _____

8. What is the plural form of bus? _____

OnBoard Academics Workbook Grade 3 ELA

Suffixes and Spelling

Key Vocabulary

Suffix

CVC word

CCVC word

Sometimes adding a suffix can change the spelling of the root word.

Put an X in the circle when you identify the difference. Put a check mark in the circle if there is no difference.

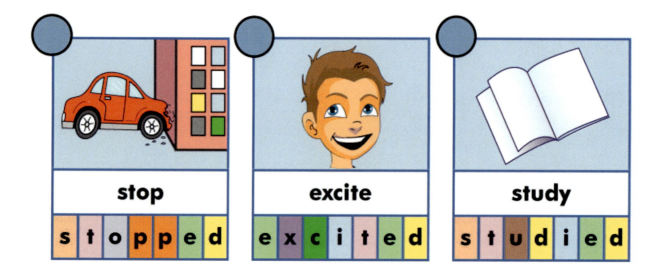

Are the root word and the suffix combination correct?

CVC=Consonant Vowel Consonant
CCVC=Consonant Consonant Vowel Consonant

When adding the suffix -ed or -ing to a CVC or CCVC word, the final consonant of the root word needs to be **doubled**.

cut + ing = ~~cuting~~ → **cutting**

flip + ed = ~~fliped~~ → **flipped**

OnBoard Academics Workbook

Grade 3 ELA

Build the missing words.

Use the colored boxes at the bottom to build your answers.

James _____ his foot to the beat.

The cat _____ at the ball of yarn.

I was _____ at the end of the play.

Grace was _____ with Jenna.

| bat | chat | clap | tap | ed | ing | p | t |

When adding a suffix beginning with a vowel to a word ending with -e, the final -e of the root word is dropped.

care + ed = ca~~re~~ed → **cared**

live + ing = liv~~e~~ing → **living**

Sort the words.

correct spelling

incorrect spelling

createed   caring   exciting

blameed   wasteing   placed

When adding **-ed** or **-es** to a word ending with **-y**, drop the -y and add an **-i** to the root word.

carry + ed = ~~carryed~~ → **carried**

story + es = ~~storyes~~ → **stories**

Add the suffix to make a new word.

carry + ed = _____

story + es = _____

sky + es = _____

party + es = _____

apply + ed = _____

puppy + es = _____

OnBoard Academics Workbook Grade 3 ELA

Identify the sentence with the correct spelling by putting a check mark in the box.

1	Owen has traveled to ten cityes.	☐
2	My mom dropped me off at school	☐
3	The woman siped her soda.	☐
4	David hurried to his desk.	☐
5	My sister likeed her new toy.	☐
6	The dog was siting on the floor.	☐

Name_____

Suffixes and Spelling Quiz
Circle the correct answer.

1. The correct plural of pony is ponyes. True or false.

2. The boy was _____ to first base.
   runing running runnning runeing

3. I _____ my wish would come true.
   hopped hopes hoped hooped

4. We were _____ the soccer ball.
   chaseing chasing chaysing chaseng

5. The coach _____ his hands.
   waving waveing waved wavd

6. We _____ for the team.
   claped clapped clapping claping

7. It was an _____ game!
   exciteing excited excitd exciting

8. I found three _____ on the floor.
   pennys pennyes pennies penny

Fluency

Key Vocabulary

fluency

speed

accuracy

intonation

context

OnBoard Academics Workbook Grade 3 ELA

Fluency is the ability to read text with the proper speed, accuracy and intonation.

Roses are red
Violets are blue
Sugar is sweet
And, so are you

Read the poem three different ways.
Put a check in the circle when you achieved description below. If possible read to another person and ask them if you achieved the description

slow and impassive

normal and fluent

fast and hard to understand

Does the conversation fit with the **context** and the **punctuation?**

"Do you see what I see?"

"It's snowing outside!"

"Let's make a snowman."

Would it be correct to read the above passage in a very slow and boring fashion? Try it and see.

Context and Punctuation

A good pace sounds like natural conversation, a nd the correct intonation would help us to understand that the boys are excited...Look for clues in **context and punctuation.**

OnBoard Academics Workbook Grade 3 ELA

Punctuation and Fluency

> **Punctuation marks** indicate how a sentence should be read.

Read the sentence and use the punctuation in red as a clue to the way it should be read.

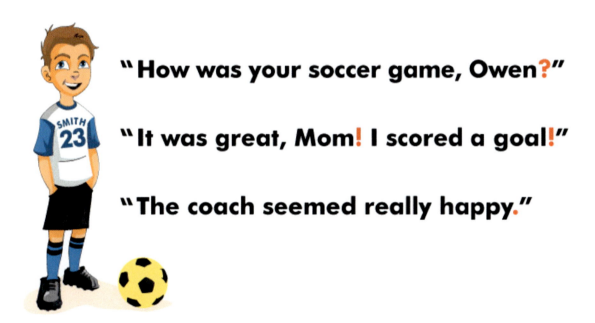

"How was your soccer game, Owen?"

"It was great, Mom! I scored a goal!"

"The coach seemed really happy."

Use context and punctuation clues to fill in the missing words.

Action verbs such as *shouted*, *roared*, and *whispered* give clues to the intonation of a sentence.

"Don't run with scissors!" his mother [ ].

The airplane engines [ ] into life.

"The baby is sleeping," the boy [ ].

roared   whispered   shouted

Name_____

Fluency Quiz

1. Fluency is the ability to read text with proper speed, accuracy and intonation. True or false?

2. Action verbs give clues to the intonation of a sentence. True or false?

3. Punctuation marks are not helpful to someone reading a story. True or false?

OnBoard Academics Workbook — Grade 3 ELA

Newburyport, MA 01950

1-800-596-3175

OnBoard Academics employs teachers to make lessons for teachers! We create and publish a wide range of aligned lessons in math, science and ELA for use on most EdTech devices including whiteboard, tablets, computers and pdfs for printing.

All of our lessons are aligned to the common core, the Next Generation Science Standards and all state standards.

If you like our products please visit our website for information on individual lessons, teachers licenses, building licenses, district licenses and subscriptions.

Thank you for using OnBoard Academic products.

Made in the USA
Middletown, DE
19 October 2023